WHY DOES MY BODY DO THAT?

SWEAT

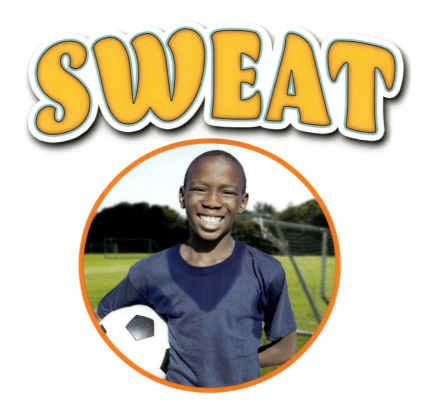

by Rachel Rose

Consultant: Beth Gambro
Reading Specialist, Yorkville, Illinois

Minneapolis, Minnesota

Teaching Tips

Before Reading

- Look at the cover of the book. Discuss the picture and the title.
- Ask readers to brainstorm a list of what they already know about sweating. What can they expect to see in this book?
- Go on a picture walk, looking through the pictures to discuss vocabulary and make predictions about the text.

During Reading

- Read for purpose. Encourage readers to think about sweating as they are reading.
- Ask readers to look for the details of the book. What are they learning about the body and how it sweats?
- If readers encounter an unknown word, ask them to look at the sounds in the word. Then, ask them to look at the rest of the page. Are there any clues to help them understand?

After Reading

- Encourage readers to pick a buddy and reread the book together.
- Ask readers to name two things that can cause sweating. Find the pages that tell about these things.
- Ask readers to write or draw something they learned about sweating.

Credits: Cover and title page, © AfricaImages/iStock and © MojanB/iStock; 3, © fizkes/Shutterstock; 5, © FatCamera/iStock; 6–7, © gjohnstonphoto/iStock; 9, © Henadzi Pechan/iStock; 11, © New Africa/Shutterstock; 12–13, © katleho Seisa/iStock; 14–15, © monkeybusinessimages/iStock; 17, © Leonard Mc Lane/iStock; 18–19, © atsurkan/Shutterstock; 21, © junce/iStock; 22C, © russaquarius/iStock; 22R, © Tetiana Lazunova/iStock; 23TL, © SciePro/iStock; 23TC, © fotokostic/iStock; 23TR, © Joaquin Corbalan/iStock; 23BL, © fizkes/iStock; 23BC, © PixieMe/Shutterstock; and 23BR, © kazoka30/iStock.

Library of Congress Cataloging-in-Publication Data is available at www.loc.gov or upon request from the publisher.

ISBN: 978-1-63691-823-5 (hardcover)
ISBN: 978-1-63691-830-3 (paperback)
ISBN: 978-1-63691-837-2 (ebook)

Copyright © 2023 Bearport Publishing Company. All rights reserved. No part of this publication may be reproduced in whole or in part, stored in any retrieval system, or transmitted in any form or by any means, electronic, mechanical, photocopying, recording, or otherwise, without written permission from the publisher.

For more information, write to Bearport Publishing, 5357 Penn Avenue South, Minneapolis, MN 55419. Printed in the United States of America.

Contents

Dripping Sweat 4

See It Happen 22

Glossary 23

Index 24

Read More 24

Learn More Online 24

About the Author 24

Dripping Sweat

I love to run and play.

But when I do, something happens.

My face gets wet.

Drip, drop!

Why does my body do that?

Everybody sweats.

People often sweat when they are hot.

It helps the body cool down.

But how does it happen?

First, your **brain** tells your body to sweat.

Sweat is made inside your skin.

It comes out through little holes called **pores**.

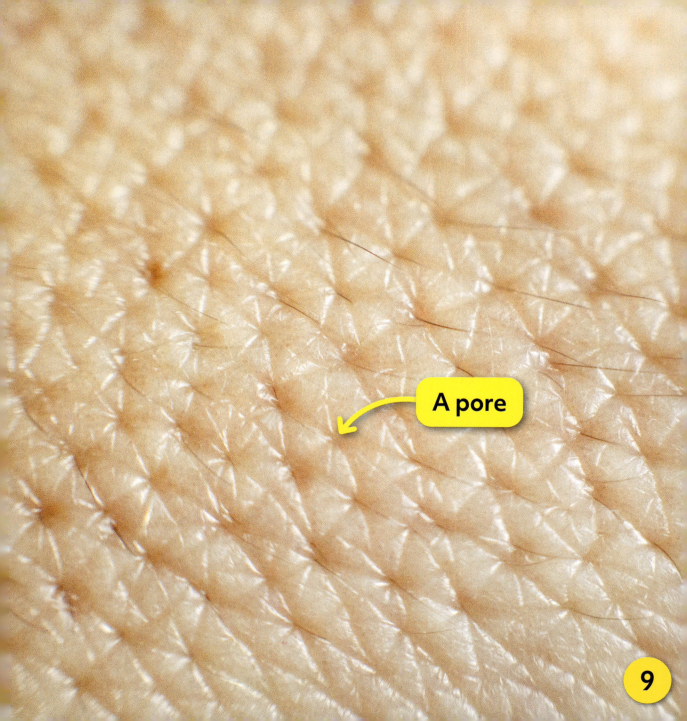

Then, air dries the sweat on your body.

It changes the **liquid** into a **vapor**.

This cools your skin.

Pee-yew!

Sometimes, people stink after they sweat.

But sweat does not smell.

As it dries, sweat mixes with other things on your skin.

That makes the stink.

Many things make you sweat.

It can happen when you **exercise** a lot.

You can sweat when you are in the sun a long time.

Sometimes, people sweat when they are **nervous**.

Their hands can get wet with sweat.

Does this ever happen to you?

Sweat is made of mostly water.

So when you sweat, your body loses water.

Be sure to drink water after you sweat.

Gulp!

Some people sweat a little.

Others sweat a lot.

It is good to sweat.

Sweating means your body is healthy.

Have fun and get sweaty!

See It Happen

When you are too hot, your brain tells your body to sweat.

Sweat is made inside the skin.

It comes out through pores.

Air turns sweat to vapor. This cools you down.

Glossary

brain the part of the body that tells other parts what to do

exercise to move your body in order to stay healthy

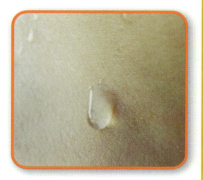

liquid a thing that flows and has no shape, such as water

nervous worried or scared

pores tiny holes in the skin

vapor something in the form of a gas

Index

air 10, 22
brain 8, 22
exercise 14
pores 8–9, 22
skin 8, 10, 12, 22
sun 14
vapor 10, 22
water 18

Read More

Capicola, Anthony. *Sweat (Your Body at Its Grossest).* New York: Gareth Stevens, 2018.

Hansen, Grace. *Sweat (Gross Body Functions).* Minneapolis: Abdo Kids, 2021.

Learn More Online

1. Go to **www.factsurfer.com** or scan the QR code below.
2. Enter "**Sweat**" into the search box.
3. Click on the cover of this book to see a list of websites.

About the Author

Rachel Rose lives in California. She loves to go hiking with her pup. Sometimes, this makes her sweat . . . a lot!